The Job

The Job

AGLUPPOS

ISBN: 978-951-98911-5-6 (paperback)
ISBN: 978-951-98911-6-3 (ePub)

Stone's rolling on the graveyard,
the baroque standard lamps stand by the naked paths
and the surveillance cameras spy blue collars
drawing lines to the sand with Fiskars rakes

I wander behind the bell tower on rock
it is firm against the soles, it will take it
I pull a cigarette secretly, I cough
like on a train they thunder past the village,
the faces and voices
past the wood in their miserable cars

It is a strange whistle stop now, still here I am
even if it doesn't concern me
or really anyone else either
particularly it does not concern my wallet
which remains empty as this widely deserted garden

and this blank, dull day

they still wage wars beyond the frontiers

and they eat cactuses in the slums behind the sea

and there are bedbugs in our tomatoes

O how this flat, pointless grass rings

whose mind could it calm in the hell anyway

and in the heaven they don't miss it

with their harps and *pling plong*

This originated ages ago: they started to die

and as plague wreaked havoc

and the breaking wheels got crowded

they set up a stone quarry

and commenced hiding corpses under granite

There are them aplenty here alright

and all with personal epitaphs,

as the office's brochure describes

the letters are provided with golden borders, or without

But now let's quit kidding, this is the valley of sorrow

the weeds must be expelled from the banks

so the cadavers do not take offence and rise at night,

to scratch plantains from their resting places

I look at the work machines

scythe would be best for that bank

but chief wants to hear the betraying blatting,

to track the blue collars

Listen, this is hard biz, no slacking

Right, nope, right, nope

I wonder how big a sledgehammer one needs

to properly mineralize those suckers

when petrol runs out, I laugh

just like the pitched, dry bore in the desert

I visit the city, I try to blow this stink from my skull

I walk and register, stone and board goods

here's another pile

I ponder where it might be going

I sit and watch folks,

Today

I had the privilege to dig

with a magnificent hangover, and I discovered

six uncanny soft brown, round objects

under the soil (from the old territory)

got malicious thump to the spade, and as I wavered

the sexton cursed

now give that here goddamnit

I passed it to him, by all means, take, please

there's more where that came from

we piled them on a handsome hill under the fir twigs

I suggested to take one of the cuties to the coffee break

for old times' sake, but it didn't amuse

our Lady Comrade at all, lousy coffee company, I suppose

Later in the afternoon I showed my dear chick

one vertebra, just as she wanted

she almost puked

meh, I returned it to the grave grove, not quite

at its proper place

and very soon the transgressor felt ashamed

and worried if the violated ones would come

and haunt his dreams, bring grey hair and blood bursts

(they came)

Well anyhow, here I sit and watch

as the vehicle is not arriving, I await in a bar,

the goons tell me this is a most infamous place,

the autopiano will rumble when one puts a fiver to it

I drop a fiver to the slot and sit, and drink,

not to enjoy the taste but to avoid falling behind

I try to suck enough before the bus leaves

all the positions are equally excellent

I change seats

Näsinneula tower visible through the window,

with city dwellers erranding on the streets

they have sun lenses now, it's summer you see

no leather jackets any more

like in spring every single person wore

The anarchists and the green assemble today,

I wish you luck,

beware of the cops

AND UNSHACKLE THE HENS, AND

THE HORSES AND ALL THE LIVING BEINGS

at the bus station it is sunny,

and clear, as the weather is dry

near the bus doors there are men
standing doing nothing,
industriously,

Also I remember how I travelled, back then
with all the seven hundred years exploited again (they fled)
on an agora when those vomited out of the pubs
had their swigs on their way back
TO THEIR BIZARRE TWINKLE EYED NIGHTS
(WHICH WERE REALLY DAYS,
THE WITHERED STATEMENT OF
THE COLLECTOR OF CURIOSITIES)

I'm sure no one figured that out
but yes, you know those Rimbaud-literate punks
on the backyards of stations, the beaming ghosts
who have rummaged through all the parties
and licked all pussies and swept the
bottom of every single gutter and slept in jail and asserted:
WE LIVE

Bugger

the deacon devils are coming this way,

do I have time to hide, no

they yearn to help after they heard our money is scarce,

I am so temped to kick them to their kneecaps

oh you poor thing, let us *help* you

how they would rejoice if they were allowed

to donate a bagful of pastries

Please, you do not understand

in this village we have so few of you poor wretches

the *vibes* we get from giving!

and our assistant sextoness

that strange concoction of sledge user and seamstress

she wanted to help me most intimately,

she asked to carry me in her renovated Buick

TO LOOK AT HER FURNITURE

Wish that car runs over the sexton

I hope with a good conscience, he said once, you know

when a Camaro almost lucked,

Oh, that was a close call,

such a joyous corpse you were about to get

And that measly hag, that vintage slime, Lady Comrade

wanders a slide rule in her pocket,

measures minutes to the next coffee break,

she manages flowerbeds, she left her home, so she tells,

once upon a time in search for money to claim her own,

came here to spend a year

and stayed a decade, poor Lady Lost

Nowadays she is bound to go ballistic over trifles

she fights over power with the sexton

and never gets it

but she can still bully us with her tongue,

she wraps it around our heads

and over our ears, she hexes us, she homogenizes

When the free birds sing

and the mind soars

like the rake by the sunny, red ochre wall

she strikes! - hauls herself after you and flows

slowly over your head

Its *so* hot,

Watch it

You will loose that zeal

Yes, that is so,

You see,

Namely so

I now keep a stash of bog roll in my pocket

I roll earplugs from it

I AM WAITING FOR A NEW SPRING,

AND IT WILL COME

OR THE END OF THE WORLD, IT -

PERHAPS THESE STONES

RISE TO WALK NEXT NIGHT, PERHAPS

THE INFATUATED GRASS WILL SURGE SOON,

perhaps you will take my mind from me

All the movements hasten the dubious outcome

gravel rolls in the slope,

my voice carries beyond the night

there is still some future left

every single step wears its sole

and when this day has run dry,

I will vanish into my hut in the grove

do not come

Again

I am startled awake

as the sun hits its needles into my eyes

infuses this foliage with fire

eye splits open

one step,

and I descend to the valley, to count the stones and to dig

In the café

there is a phone booth,

a slimy prism all quiet, no tinkle

in Camaro are the dudes with their pop machines

thump, thuddy, thud: life on debt

heck, let's just steal

they are about to face a wall

on top of which are sitting the ancient Elders who state

you shall not pass

The Old, chained to rock,

the windless, sneezy heroes

utter their foul vocabulary silently, in all seriousness

I also want a new tomorrow

and a player and into it ten metric tons of Ministry

Crows, friends in their black capes

ranting in spruces

caw, caw,

awk,

I clap my hands and they quieten to listen

Get back to work!

the sexton roars,

Move

No sitting there

I wasn't sitting, dammit

I have pushed this mower

for two hours now, I thought

I pant a little on the pretext that I am filling this basin

he looks sideways

and then comes to whisper

listen, I don't mind

even if you rest sometimes, I am not a monster but

not when there are people here

do you mean the woman who was just here, yes

Did you know

that EMOTION does not move stone,

hide that warmer hand to the pocket
bite your jawbone, now we tackle the real waltz
O Fiskars

The sexton heard, felt, calculated, that is, he inferred
everything in his youth
he calculated the odds like Pascal and invested in the eternity
apprentices such an ancient doctrine
and now he speaks the lexicon of stone to us
and grinds mere chaff and scabs to our soles

No matter
this is the real deal, the master league
the sexton is familiar with the charm of the absolute power,
he tells us
about the graves to which the church has sold eternal care
But from those care contracts though -
What about them?
One should get rid of.
Oh, how can you do that?
By annulling the agreement one-sidedly,
he says and grins

In the afternoon, Zeke personally, the chief executive

of all the cemeteries of the city comes to scold

come here, got something to tell you

I am walked into the cool of the parish meeting hall

to confront a full jury, very serious

you have reputedly been loafing

no I have not

and been telling women what to do with it

seriously not

I've already formed an opinion

         about you take care it doesn't -
(right, just as me about you)

I will indeed start dawdling,

if this is the name of the game

I return home,

I wonder what has happened meanwhile

I can see the transformations

but how morphs all that I cannot see

the job, the family, a child,

this all was chosen just out of curiosity

would you like, the woman asked, I don't know

what will it be like, I asked

you will find out

fine

So we got our stuff together and started moving

as car combat trucks, on adjacent rails,

pedal to the metal and machine gun

resounding in the face every day

that's the spirit

the heat dissipates as the years add up

not giving up yet, though

Is it an expedition, one which cannot be excused?

Are you still aboard? How about your camera? Broke it?

Yes, I'll try to explain to myself,

what I'm doing here

I invent a good tale, really quite fine

Night falls over us and in the morning

I will leave the explanation behind and step forward

(as you aren't going anywhere else)

watch: and what you see is altered,

the attempt to describe remains an attempt

and that is all you got, a fragment

This is a silent

the sun falls from its track

the adventure looses its momentum and sticks in a marsh

and nothing is real but Revolution

(do not trust that either;

do not expect a blow from the anticipated direction:

the one who then hits you, cheats)

I eat canned food, cardboard, anything I have here

I am scornful, witty and resourceful, I play chess

I put a gas mask over my face and stuff the plugs in my ears,

I pass by, rattling

yes we are building this country

with the healthy hobbies

we fight the old men, we sit in the pool caves

get drunk and throw sticks

put on black tights and

engage in rhythmic physical exercise, martial arts mayhem

Earth and Moon

Rest comes as part of seven day series,

attention, at ease, Earth chasing Moon

around wanton axis thrown into space
(the breathers will be paid the next day)
you have the night
I have the day
no, wait
it's night here too

In the evening, together
we relocate equipment and microbes, chick and dude, thus
and then we go watch the BOX or knock the backs
of the books hunching peevishly in the shelf : hello
browse through a page or two,
and slip into slumber
(yes, yes, your embroidered worlds were retrieved
but OUR genius is unrivalled)

To the voids,
prominences, dreams
ha ha ha
nothing is permanent, still everything is still the same
such is Revolution,
I am altered just like you, and the nipper
the henchman of the chaos, two years old in our time line

That little boy,

I cannot see, the motion is too quick to be sensed

AS THE MOTION OF STONES

AS THE SPEED OF PLANTS

I stand on a deserted station, my compass filled with water

at some aloof rails, far from the WIDER paths

and somewhere out there

are the Whitecaps

No bearing

only environments I find likeable

this morning the light arrives again unchanged

and the rational monkey escapes

into his caves to scrape lottery tickets

and his old, blood-red drawings with steel wool

DID YOU SEE

THE FERTILE LAND, YOU INFIDEL DOGS?

The colleague

sits in the cockpit, shakes according to the laws of mechanics

I am tailing, I handle hydraulic arms and change my spot

MY EYE RESPONDS TO THE PRESSING OF THE

PEDAL! I AM STEEL, I AM VULGARIZED RUBBER

AND SIMULTANEOUSLY
THE BALANCE INDICATOR KNOCKS NUMISMATICS
TO THE RIGHT EDGE OF MY COGNIZANCE!
(just rust in peace the small nagging appliance
which I tried to lose carefully, somewhere, to forge
the question of why and whereto from here)

And finally,
after countless steps I can lower my hand
to a device manufactured by anonymous machinery
which I connect
as part of the industry that is my life and say:
this is MINE

In the pale green sea of buds
the elder lady from the village
a priestess (the cleric's missus) passes by, stinking
of old habsburgian fragrance and surely does not remember
how many drops of sweat and frogman's skins were required
to raise her goo from a sunken galeas

From the hill one can see the hinterlands
lead-grey lake, devoid of swimmers

sucked for drinking water to the fallen, to the stalks of grass,
to the framed roses, to the transceding trees
amidst where the tractor is dancing its insane dance

Behind the bell tower the bunnies
are bounding happily in the heather
while on the road the motorists bound forward
or maybe backwards, as time is just an agreement,
they look very small and somehow
helpless (hospital beds also boast with wheels)

I just do this
sure aren't Hungarian aluminium sledges these here
and the extremes of heat, and the sparkling light
and the soil is so hard
like fossilized bone and tractor tires, the spade thumps
to the dense bottom under a thin lump layer,

Hey, boy! laugh the hoes in their Chevies
laughs King Whopper on his way to the world
when you have torn bark from those birches
enter, and forget
enter the world

when the machines have traversed these lands,
and left their traces, absorbed oat, nectar and fragrances,
so that now, my friend
(you may not notice, but you walk on an ancient land)

the soil is brittle
and lifeless
and the dreams of mountains harden to stone and talk to you
like the Originals talk at night

Yes, we strive for ecological friendliness
Good, then you know
mulch would be perfect for those -
he pretends not to hear, walks farther - JUST SAYING
THAT FOR THOSE BUSHES, BARK MULCH -
he sneers, quarrels with Lady Comrade,
the matron lifts the tank on her back and starts to spray

A short coffee party
in memory of the man who dropped off a scaffold
after the devotional, cake and gingerbread, the cleric
gets up to lead the chanting, man in his fifties, bald,
white square covering the apple

a docile teddy bear robe hiding the hot temper

The village patriarchs stare
at the summer helps
at this undisciplined, incompetent plastic generation,
they watch
searching for a grip and tire
this weather taxes resources, the youngsters know
(and still hardly on their trip yet)
bit of cake, hymn and away
what? the birds chanting too, scoundrels
with their toothless mouths?

At the stop
I am waiting
with my honourable bag beside me
this fatigue, this repose, these rare eternities
are, and will be paid
with the sweat of seventy times seven days
there's a salt stone for you, you lick that
AND WE RUSH TO THE STREETS, TO THE PARKS
TO DANCE TO SHAKE TO SWAY
INTO THE MEMORY BOMB BLUE HAZE

You bastards

ready to fly, comrade, wings cut,

Friday night fever in Tula or Tampere or Wherever

I WAS ABOUT TO SOAR!

I ATE FROGS FOR SUPPER, I TRAVELLED WITH MY

BODY UNVEILED THROUGH THE FIERY NOON

I WAS A SHREWD MADCAP, I SAVED MY WORLD

I GLIDED OVER THE EASTERN SEA, I WAS

THE LEADER OF ONE THOUSAND BIRDS,

I WAS BEYOND THE CLOUDS IN THE BURNING

SKY, I WAS AN APE IN THE DEPTHS OF SUMMER

The night turns its blind eye on us

twangg, the mad

voodoo popper plays obscure French porn pop

with two pastel soft tit guitars

hanging around his neck, I marvel what that suggests

I have been now

awake since three

the stones were dreaming me and I woke flinching:

no rest for me in the darkness, any more?

Let me be a barnacle

at the feet of stones, let me be

a flea at flea market in the land of plantains

YOU, THE GUILTY ONE, COME OUT! I shout

the chick kicks me out of bed: get busy, let me sleep

(duller than her television

slower than her car)

but this is not a fair game

or is this a game

YOU BLUDGEONED ME WITH WOOD,

SHATTERED TO THE SEASHORE,

THERE I SOLD MY PRECIOUS TIME AND LEFT,

TO BUY IT BACK AS SMALL FRAGMENTS

later on, these times will be different

Not doing too well if you start liking work like this,

comrade says first thing in the morning

HOW SPACE AND DIMENSIONS

FLOW WHEN YOU WALK

a howling piece of world hurls from the radio into my lap,

"however, a piece of three metres was snapped

in a March storm", was written in it

I JOURNEYED TO THE MOON
DURING THE COFFEE BREAK
in what storm,
I do not know,
I have not heard
is there a storm here

I cannot repair the dreams
turned over by the furiously flailing branches
the sexton fucks with me, says
that my missus likes me for sure
how so
since you do everything so slowly

on the road, toddlers
shamble to the Sunday school
such a strange village

And the chosen ones
marry to fuck the fellows of the Cross
thinking only about it, on tables,

on leather sofas on a Sabbath,
on holy divans, fuck the fellows of the Cross,
wear their brown skin like shampoo

On office tables
pushing erasers, rubber bands, binders, and phones to the
floor and fuck fellows of the Cross,
groaning on the linoleum, hunting for you
to rush to the green sources, to spread over all earth,
and they know intimately your woman who is Fertility
in their arched office residing in utter silence
(and I traced you
to the sunset, all in vain)
as the fire and the world in us
and we have two worlds
and we were given The Choice and The Equation
and in the equation there were a billion unknown stars
and we made our decision

I go to a gas station
and have a coffee, I look at the video games
living dead are blasted there
they seem to splash into smithereens just like anyone else

the air returns everything, nothing sticks to it just try

our last joke, and you don't have a clue

you lungfish

let us burn the Earth

scorch with fire into dwellings,

let the smith forge in his workshop wonders for the markets

while we fall, torn, through the fluffy air

In the evening on the streets

the work goes on

the walk method will probably lead somewhere

(meticulously, left, and right - it is an advantage)

(as a stranger here, quite without bounds, unwilling to return

to retrace to the crossing

where you stepped on the roadless and went astray)

women whose wombs are waiting for the seed

whose lips curve to a smile

a plastic bag rustles

in man's hand, in the bag a lonely melon

the man weighs too much, his trainers bruise asphalt,

don't you remember how I helped you, the sea asks

no, the man replies

On the bus

a skinny girl gnaws an apple, quietly, timidly

crosses her arms and sleeps

only in her dreams she has might and grace

when the truck drivers trample through all her days

and we,

when we ask for a home

we are given one hundred metres of corrugated titanium

although we do not know what it is,

or what we should do with it

my head aches

the storm is coming,

They will soon rope us to the roof,

to guide the union of heaven and earth

back together and whole

for as the ring does not break

so will not break the strongest link of the chain

comrade in the afternoon

comrade in the sun of the afternoon,

hurries through the series of movements, disappears

comrade knows well

when we will end up as lightning rods on the roof ridge

he has worked long and hard on these lands, very long

old hardy, he knows

Now Lady Comrade has snitched on old hardy,

said he has been idling on the site

he was promptly demoted to clean rose bushes

the tractor weeps black diesel tears in the shed

man longs for his grease nipples

(I have never loitered at work, it's all bullshit!)

I walk under spruces, I look at an ant hill,

they build and then some more, have one second breaks,

what are they thinking

(who has passed through these paths

who has toiled these monotonous gestures

for decades, knows the steps and can tell the rhythm

it must be possible, You can't tire so easily

those too are still moving

they are alive, roughly)

The sparrows twitter in the bushes, they inform

from that hyperdupermall you can find sunflower seeds

the sexton

clothes himself in his dwarven stockiness and grins

(he noticed me exiting the thicket)

stealing time I see

and pushing the carts with *such* a diligent look, he mocks

He comes to mess up along,

gives advices and swings the tool

like an ordinary man

(for the sake of fitness you know,

while you inspect and trade quips)

then he grabs a machine and wanders around the fields

while others are pulling harrows

   look now he mucks up all the paths

   right, so what are you gonna do?

I adjust pebbles, decorate flower nests,

spray mowers, hit the gas and no fingers to the blades

scrupulously and rapidly, straighten headstones,

300 kilos of granite barely misses the metatarsuses

the decoration is pried back up

we start looking for remnants of the geraniums

and still the larder appears to be empty

it is empty

Do you realize

without compromising the thought the heart the arms

fall in poem, fall in thinking, merely fall

I am here just leaving traces, so

STEPS IN THE SAND, SUCCUMB!

STEPS ON THE COASTLINE,

EARN THE ETERNAL GREEN BEYOND!

STEPS BY THE EDGE OF SPACE, COME TO US

WHEN THE STONES ARE COVERED

WITH WRITING! (and they will)

And still we share the seats in the same lifeboat

somewhere,

in the midst of its nature, the monkey sleeps

and wanders

insanely happy:

I AM BRILLIANT! I HAVE DISCOVERED!

I AM ALIVE! AND HEAR, O blind,

deaf and numb!

your bright blade has hit the darkness!

Do you still expect us to decipher

your math homework with you? WRONG

your enumerable days, what are they to me? my

imaginary lights are interspersed among the calculated ones

and decree the number and substance of them, their bearing

Perhaps these steps will disappear without a trace

do I wish them engraved to this rock, no

it will not happen, the waters come and go

tone the muscles and retard their genius

no, that will hardly come to pass

I see myself too surprised in the mirror

I descend in the current deeper , every day

dozing,

I wake up when my bus spits me out watyumbleh -

In the city there is a chick who has mid-calf boots

and mini skirt

and she sits on the opposite to change her flea market boots

legs spread out and boy she really takes her time

good old city

the gloomy, old, proper shit pile

well, we came here to cheat time,

there is no degeneration here, at these crossroads

and if incidentally there is, it is disguised as a babyface

O city, press me between your tits

you can be old, I don't care

(I can hear

how her nails reach out far, groping

dirt and life and the sun and time

from where it is so swift it seems stopped)

Tonight I will walk again

imagine I went to play heliotropic bridge

if it makes you feel more beautiful

there is sort of truth to it

I move my feet around in smoky rooms and clank my mugs

in search for glitter

are there bombs in the jukebox?

who's gonna blow my mind?

can I sell my my gland buzz today?

hey, can I get some heavenly light here please

that

is heliotropism

Ask by all means,

only you don't really want answers

but answers that sound lovely

and I perform already pretty well I think,

break patterns at times, slake lime and mummify

stay steadfastly in bed

(oh, how I slept in again today ...and the nap...)

The calendar was invented in courtesan's embrace

AND WE ARE BREEZE

AND WILLOWHERB CANDY FLOSS

AND FANTASIES OF THE AIR

and there is a Letter in my dream

and in that letter there is a stroke in the stone

I bend down to study the writing

and right away someone hurries by me and cries: HEY,

come to play with us!

he has a doomsday device under his arm, levers and joints

I am still, I watch, and wait, and see how the cry

gets written to the stone

I rise exactly the right time, I continue my journey, frolic

I pull trucks with my teeth, spoon the bitter soup

from the same bowls as others, cross out to mark,

and simultaneously I sense how

IN THE SILENCE OF THE FOREST THE STONE

WRITES ITS WILD LONELINESS

never responds although all to the woods cry

go there, my friends (and the rest of you, especially)

Take the time machine

see, your bayonets are all rusty

bury them in the ground,

or you drive them through your guts

do you hear me (my love)

this is the spoken language of the stone

these sentences can break darning needles

perhaps you know:

if you pace on a cliff, your feet will get its shape

but how can YOU walk with such impeccable ease??

Difficult to see

yesterday I visited the old man's house,

there were relatives there

I saw such a reproachful silence in the eyes of my cousin

when she recognized a consanguinity

something memorable, which has been forgotten

carelessly, deliberately

(it's all fabrication for me and nothing more, so foreign)

Today we are among ourselves,

the armours are sleeping by the road and it's a warm,

mirror calm evening of June

you carry a glass of wine with you as we talk

and the children are swimming

and we are catching up with reality

they run, three girls over a long pier

　　　　　headlong into the lake　　*splash, splash,*

　　　　　　　　　　　　　　　　　　　splash

more children on another side of the strait,

three as well, they dive likewise

I will remember this

when I am gone my memory will persist

and keep carrying this with you

and I will remember:

I too was here

this I would tell up against the eternity

if the divine herald came to me, to state: your words will stay

that I TOO WAS HERE

Stroke

in the colours in the sounds in gravitation our dreams

in the virtuous thoughts, in the wicked ones

and after you are crammed

through the omnipresent crystal shredder

you can hardly discern one from the other

In the soft curves of breast

in booze jugs, stars long neglected by gods

our sleep

when they come to inquire do not listen to what they say

be mindful, they are writing to the stone just like you

and most importantly,

ANSWER VERY SLOWLY

AS IF IT INDEED

HAD SOME SIGNIFICANCE TO YOU

The crow swarm takes flight

from an old, wooden (abandoned) pharmacy

behind the chemist's shop there is the lake,

it is large and hundreds of church boats have cut through it

back when we still worshipped

the ground the cleric walked on, and listened
to the BIG voice

A woman and a man rise from the shore,
in the gentle willowherb candy floss rain
the woman with young, blue hair
the man with shaken, grey power, he glances fuzzily around
with a resemblance to a hastily dressed coat
if I only had a small craft here and on a thwart a kantele
and the large inland lake before me, like an ash-grey storm

Thunder
is it still that severe Dude
of the midsummer? Or the one more tired,
aged August rumble drawing away?
No - He still hurls hammers,
listen, how the air the monkey breathes,
breaks, and boils

See how it tears its way, in angular lines,
vertically up from the ground towards the ink blue clouds
for which, by the way
we still do not have wings

I am sitting

and listening

this is a natural way to be

to sit somewhere, to be done

preferably devoid of thoughts

the child comes

asks what are those are bugs there on the window

Well, they -

Musca domestica

Aglais urticae, Anax imperator

Coccinella septempunctata O amagad

UNSHACKLE UNSHACKLE UNSHACKLE

www.ingramcontent.com/pod-product-compliance
Lightning Source LLC
Chambersburg PA
CBHW030308030426
42337CB00012B/638